AFRICA IS EMERGING
Hard Facts About Easy Market Entry

Ndudi Osakwe

AUTHORNOMY

Africa is Emerging: Hard Facts About Easy Market Entry

Copyright © 2021 by Ndudi Osakwe

All rights reserved.

No part of this publication may be reproduced, stored in a retrieval system, or transmitted, in any form or by any means electronic, mechanical, photocopying, recording, or otherwise, without the prior permission of the author who is the copyright owner.

ISBN 978-978-995-796–5

Published by:
Authornomy Publishing
Plot 2 Block C, Oluyole Estate Extension
Ibadan, Oyo State, Nigeria
+2348036970282
authornomy@gmail.com

Contents

Preface, *v*

CHAPTER 1
Where is Africa? 9
  Gateways to Africa, 10
  The United Arab Emirates (UAE), 25
  Africa is Now, 26

CHAPTER 2
Why Should You Do Business in Africa?, 31
  The Opportunities, 32
  Africa is a Land of Opportunities, 33
  Unlocking the Opportunities, 39
  Investment Opportunities by Sector, 40
  Israel: The Game Changer, 49
  Bottlenecks, 54

CHAPTER 3
How to Enter Africa?, 57
  Preparing for Success, 58
  The Inner Game of Tennis, 59
  Preparation is Key, 62
  Identifying Local Partners 67

CHAPTER 4
Hard Facts About Easy Market Entry, 71

Further Reading, 81

About the Author, 85

Preface

I have been inspired to write this book by the need to change the perception of Africa as a monolith. Africa is a continent made up of 54 countries, each with its distinct culture, history, system of administration, language, economy, and etcetera. Therefore, understanding the character of the African space is a requirement for successfully doing business on the continent.

The story of Africa is awash with myths. While this book is not an adventure into fact-finding and verification of news about Africa, it has been written to spur interest and generate enthusiasm about Africa as a continent ready to do business.

Despite having resource-based economies with attendant headwinds, Africa has undergone a lot of changes over the years through the concerted efforts of its various governments at driving change and promoting investments to their various locales.

The good news is that the world is now

acknowledging that Africa, with its market of one billion or more people, can no longer be ignored. For instance, US president, Joseph Biden, in a video call to leaders of the African Union, reiterated the United States of America's desire to engage with Africa for greater trade relations and investment in its democratic institutions. Without a doubt, an informed investor can find the right fit as many of the perceived risks are hyped. According to one analyst, Africa is not hell and it is not heaven either. It is a continent with a big, youthful population, with cities that are booming.

It is worthy of note that, in 2019, six out of the ten fastest growing economies in the world were African. It demonstrates the willingness of governments and the determination of the African people to improve their wellbeing. According to Said Ibrahimi, CEO of Casablanca Finance City and a firm believer in Africa, though Africa has complicated economies, its future growth will be built on opportunities unique to the continent. I am as hopeful as Mr. Ibrahimi that Africa will be the motor of global growth in decades to come.

As a business researcher and spatial analyst backed by more than 20 years' experience providing support to entrepreneurs investigating the African market space for entry, I consider myself qualified to write a book of this nature.

This handbook is a culmination of many years' experience as a market entry advisor and business research consultant on Africa.

CHAPTER 1

Where is Africa?

Africa is a continent south of Europe, between the Atlantic Ocean and the Indian Ocean. Its latitude and longitude lies between 9.1021N and 18.2812E and covers a total area of 30.2 million square kilometres, which is about one-fifth of the world's land area. It is one of the seven continents, and diverse in ecology, civilizations, heritage, culture, and etcetera.

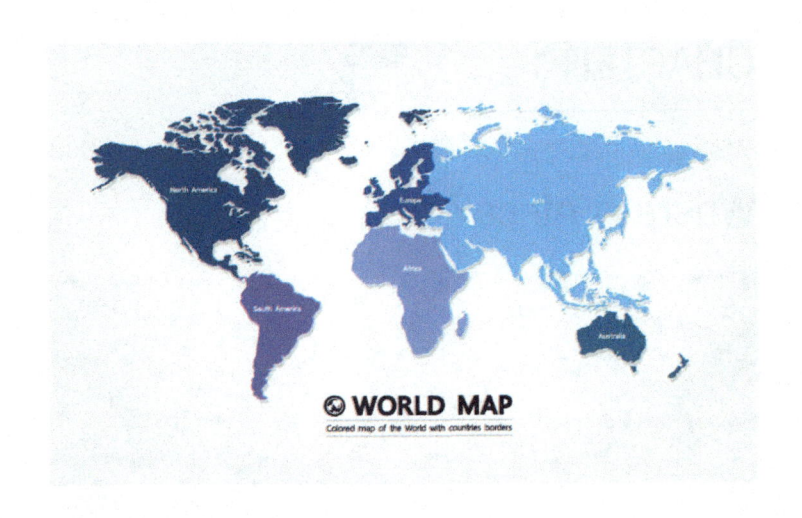

2 | *Africa is Emerging*

Africa is not a country. It is not monolithic. The physical and human spaces vary from region to region and are also diverse within regions. Africa is made up of 54 countries, with a population of about 1.3 billion people from approximately 3,000 ethnic groups. It is culturally diverse. An estimated 2,000 languages are spoken within the continent.

Where is Africa?

The countries of Africa belong to various regional economic unions, with some countries being members of more than one economic community. The blocs promote regional trade and enhance the easy movement of goods and persons.

The major economic blocs in Africa prior to African Continental Free Trade Area (AfCFTA) include the following:

- ECOWAS: Economic Community of West African States
- COMESA: Common Market for Eastern and Southern Africa
- EAC: East African Community
- SADC: South African Development Community

The regional economic blocs have coalesced into a single trade area for continent-wide integration referred to as the African Continent Free Trade Area (AfCFTA).

TEAR DOWN THE WALLS

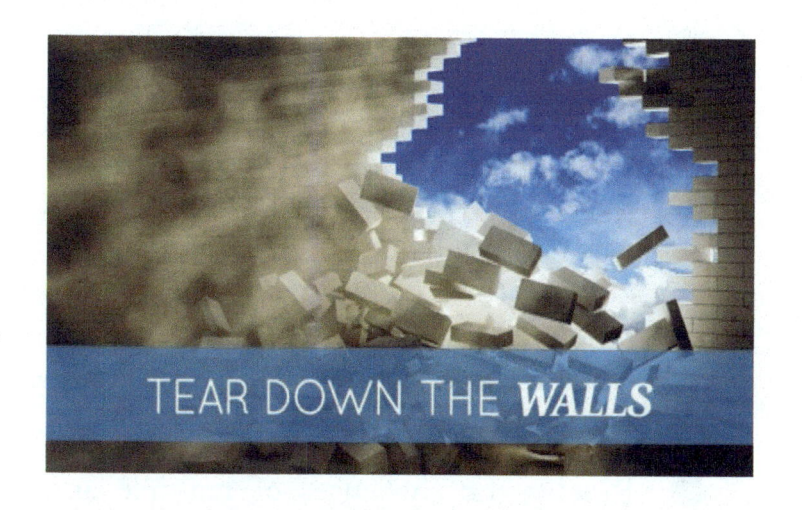

AfCFTA is the world's largest common market with a single set of trade and investment rules across a continent of 54 countries, from Egypt to South Africa, Senegal to Djibouti, with a combined GDP of over $2.5 trillion, to boost intra Africa trade, achieve economies of scale and overcome the challenges of market fragmentation.

AfCFTA falls within the strategic framework of the Africa Union Agenda 2063, which is a blueprint and master plan to transform Africa into the global powerhouse of the future. The objectives include the following:

- Create a single continental market for goods and services, with free movement of business persons and investments.

- Expand intra-African trade through better harmonization and coordination of trade liberalization and facilitation regimes and instruments across Regional Economic Communities (RECs) and across Africa in general.

- Resolve the challenges of multiple and overlapping memberships to expedite the regional and continental integration processes.

- Enhance competitiveness at the industry and enterprise level.

The message to international investors is simple: invest in one country, sell in all countries. According to a report by Rand Merchant Bank, *Where to Invest in Africa, 2019*, the following countries were ranked as top destinations in this order:

1. Egypt

2. South Africa
3. Morocco
4. Ethiopia
5. Kenya
6. Rwanda
7. Tanzania
8. Nigeria
9. Ghana
10. Ivory Coast

Cities are the engine room of economic development in countries, an indicator of the wellbeing of nations, and provide the enabling environment where connections take place, networks are built, and innovative combinations are consummated (Florida et al., 2016). A report from the New World Wealth for Mauritius based AfrBank and obtained from BusinessInsider Africa, May 10, 2021 ranked the top 10 wealthiest African cities as follows:

- Johannesburg/South Africa
- Cape Town/South Africa
- Cairo/Egypt
- Lagos/Nigeria
- Durban/South Africa
- Nairobi/Kenya
- Stellenbosch/South Africa
- Pretoria/South Africa
- Casablanca/Morocco
- Accra/Ghana

The diversity, density and cultural creativity of the urban centres serve as a major draw for startup talent. As a container of talents, the cities attract skilled persons, some of who are engaged in the growing knowledge economy and in startup ecosystems. According to StartupBlink, the top ten best startup cities in Africa in 2021 in descending order:

1. Lagos/Nigeria
2. Nairobi/Kenya
3. Cape Town/ South Africa
4. Johannesburg/South Africa
5. Cairo/Egypt
6. Kigali/Rwanda
7. Tunis/Tunisia
8. Kampala/Uganda
9. Accra/Ghana
10. Casablanca/Morocco

Connecting cities in Africa by Trans-African Highway is one of the priorities of the African Continental Free Trade Area (AfCFTA) on its road to prosperity, reports Richard Gardham (*Investment Monitor*, June, 2021).

Gateways to Africa

There are several gateways to Africa, including:

Casablanca: It is the leading financial centre in Africa. With the recent normalization of ties between Israel and Morocco, it will play a pivotal role in the promotion of trade and investment between both countries, especially through Jews of Moroccan origin. Casablanca has a stock exchange and is home to several multinational companies. It serves as a gateway to Africa, especially in reaching the Francophone countries of West Africa, including Ivory Coast and Senegal, due to shared values such as a common language, history and, in some cases, religion. The city has a burgeoning technology start-up ecosystem ranked third in North Africa, after Cairo and Tunis, according to StartupBlink, 2021. It is cosmopolitan, with French and Arabic as the official languages of the city populated mainly by people of the Islamic faith.

Office hours are between the hours of 9:00 a.m. and 5:00 p.m. The local currency is the Dirham. It has an international airport and a seaport and is home to Hassan II University. Dress code is formal. Most locals enjoy the game of football, horse riding, golf, and skiing and water sports. The popular indigenous foods include b'ssara, tagine, couscous and fish.

Information on doing business in the city and country can be obtained from the Casablanca Finance City office.

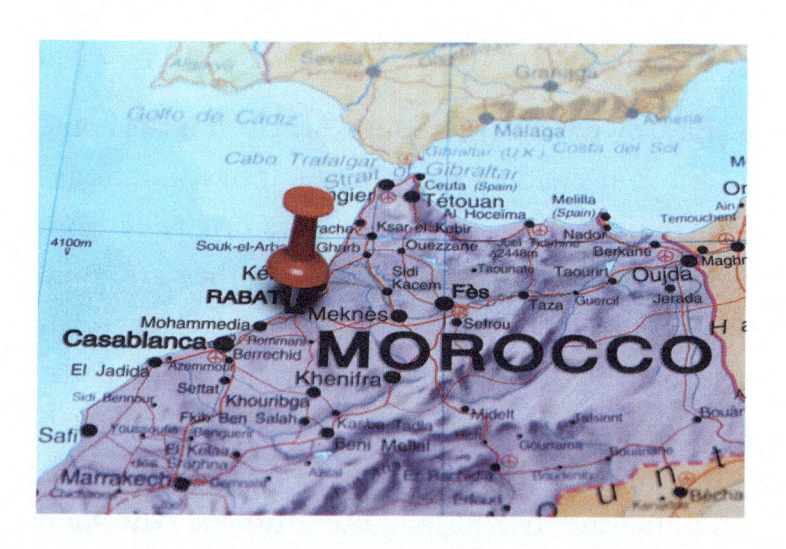

Cape Town: It is one of the top three financial centres in Africa and serves as the gateway for overseas firms from mostly English-speaking countries looking to do business in Africa. It has well-developed financial, legal, and communication sectors, and houses one of the leading technology clusters in Africa. It provides a pathway to reaching the various countries in southern Africa and occasionally serves as springboard to West Africa and other regional markets.

Cape Town is a city in South Africa. It is the home of the University of Cape Town. It has an international airport and a seaport. Jews originally from South Africa are at home here as they are quite familiar with the taste and fashion of Cape Town and South Africa in general. The city is populated by Whites, Afrikaans, Indians and few Black African. The official languages are English, Afrikaans, IsiZulu, and IsiXhosa, among others. The local currency is the Rand.

Pastimes include rugby, football, cricket, boxing, athletics, golf and tennis. Popular foods include boerewors, cape Malay curry, chakalaka, Malvasia pudding and bobotie among other local delicacies.

Office hours are usually from 9:00 a.m. to 5:00 p.m. Information about doing business in the city can be obtained from the WESGRO, the official tourism, trade and investment agency for Cape Town and the Western Cape.

Johannesburg: Known as the city of gold, Johannesburg is one of the top financial centres in Africa and is home to global companies setting foot on Africa. Like Cape Town, it is one of the preferred host cities for companies originating from English-speaking countries. With good infrastructure and an enabling environment offered by the Gauteng Growth and Development Agency (GGDA), Johannesburg presents to the world as the ultimate entry point to the rest of Africa. It has one of the most vibrant stock exchanges in Africa, and a couple of higher institutions, including the University of Johannesburg. Its signature locale for business is Sandton, renowned for meetings, incentives, conferencing and exhibitions (MICE).

Johannesburg is a city with a unique, African character, world-class infrastructure in the fields of telecommunications, transportation, water and power, and with globally-competitive healthcare and educational facilities.

South Africa is ranked 48th globally, becoming the first of African countries to reach the global top 50 technology startups ecosystem, with four ranked cities as released by StartupBlink in the *Global Startup Ecosystem Index Report, 2021*. According to the report, this could be attributed to increased private sector participation and the availability of early stage investments, thanks to forward-looking public sector initiatives.

Where is Africa? | 15

Lagos: With a population of over 20 million people, Lagos is the commercial capital of Nigeria (contributes more than 30% of its gross domestic product) and is one of the key markets in Africa serving as the principal gateway to the majority of the 15 countries in the Economic Community of West African States (ECOWAS). About 60% of expatriates in Nigeria live within the Greater Lagos Area. Though Lagos has been ranked as one of the most stressful cities in the world, it has a thriving Jewish community of over 450 families from across the world working in multinational companies or running their own businesses in the city, according to Rabbi Mendy Sternbach, Chabad of Lagos from New York, USA.

Lagos is home to several institutions of higher learning, including the University of Lagos, Yaba College of Technology, and Lagos State University, and has a growing technology ecosystem in the Yaba district. The state government has laid out plans for a major cluster for knowledge, innovation, technology and entrepreneurship (KITE) to be developed in the area. Lagos has a free trade zone and satellite cities with modern infrastructure, such as the Atlantic City on the ocean front.

Lagos is the leading technology startup ecosystem in Africa, overtaking Nairobi, and is ranked 122nd globally as a top global technology startup ecosystem as reported in a release by StartupBlink's *Global Startup Ecosystem Index Report, 2021*. The index takes into account several dozens of parameters, including the number of startups, the size of the domestic market, and the ease of doing business.

Lagos is ranked among the global top 50 cities for e-commerce and retail technology and the top 100th for transportation technology and educational technology. Lagos is home to unicorns, including Jumia, Flutterwave and several large banks with branches across Africa and the world. The local currency is the Naira.

Lagos is the melting pot of cultures. Major tribes include the Yorubas, Igbos, Hausas, with several other ethnic groups across the country. Main religions are Christianity and Islam. It has an international airport and a seaport. English is the official language. The residents give their free time to the game of football, tennis, boxing and athletics. There are golf and polo courses as well. Popular foods include rice, fufu, amala, plantain and yam. The working hours are between 8:00 a.m. and 4:00 p.m.

Information about doing business is available at the Lagos Global Office domiciled in the Governor's Office and the Nigerian Investment Promotion Commission (NIPC).

Accra: It is rapidly emerging as a city to reckon with in the West African region due to the stable political climate and the enabling environment that help in the nurture and growth of businesses in the country. It plays host to many African Americans and Diaspora Africans in the Caribbean and South America. In response to campaigns and road shows such as 'Ghana Cares,' these communities of repatriates and expatriates have helped to promote the city as an investment destination. Little wonder the country, Ghana emerged as the fastest growing economy in the world in 2019.

The Greater Accra Area is populated by locals from various tribes, including the Akan, Ewe and Mole-Dagbon. Like Nigeria, it is an English-speaking country. Other languages spoken include Asante and Fante. The religious practices are Christianity, Islam and traditional African religion. It has an international airport. The local currency is the Cedi. Pastimes include football, boxing, basketball, athletics, rugby, golf and tennis. The popular foods of the people living in the city include rice, fufu, waakye, banku and plantain.

Official working hours are between 8:00 a.m. and 4:00 p.m. Dress code is formal. Information on doing business in Accra is available at the Ghana Investment Promotion Centre.

Kigali: Kigali is a city that demonstrates resilience and the capacity of a people to overcome. It has become one of the key cities on the continent that can offer entry into other markets such as DR Congo and Angola. French and English are widely spoken in Kigali and it has emerged as a MICE city, hosting conferences on technology and innovation. Kigali is referred to as a 'test kitchen,' a great place to demo because it is a small market, easy to set up shop and especially easy to implement new concepts at a low cost, reports *Disrupt Africa*, 2019. Businesses can be registered in one day and usually at no cost to the firm. Its economy has grown largely due to a good governance structure and enabling business environment. Dubbed the most inviting city in Africa, community service (umunagana) is a way of life.

Kigali is home to several startup successes, second highest ranked startup technology city in East Africa after Nairobi, and 265th globally. Massive government support has bolstered the ecosystem, including the Entrepreneur visas for ICT startups which makes it an attractive relocation option for entrepreneurs in the region. It has an international airport and is home to several institutions of higher learning, including the University of Rwanda, University of Kigali and the Kigobora Polytechnic. The local currency is the Rwandan Franc.

Favorite pastimes include football, athletics and basketball. Popular indigenous foods include umutsima, pounded cassava leaves, mixuzu, and ubuki. Office hours are between 8:00 a.m. and 12:30 p.m. and 1:30 p.m. and 5:00 p.m. Dress code is formal to meetings and punctuality is paramount. Information on doing business in Kigali is available at the Rwanda Investment Promotion Centre.

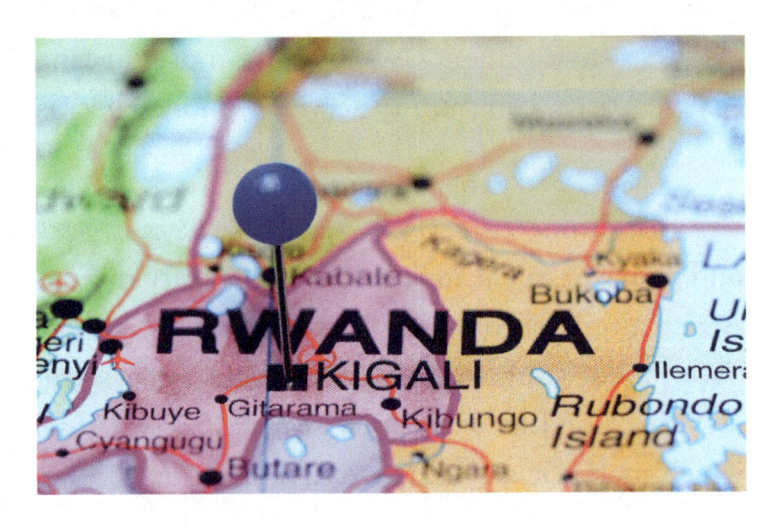

Nairobi: It is the capital of Kenya and has been identified as one of the key host countries for startups and FinTech. According to a release by StartupBlink's *Global Startup Ecosystem Index Report, 2021*, Nairobi ranks 136th place globally as a tech ecosystem and is one of the two top-ranked cities in Kenya and 61st in the global top startups ecosystem. According to the report, its growth is propelled by the innovative technology hub, especially the mobile payment solutions and the presence of global tech giants, including Google, Microsoft and Samsung among others. It is the home of M-Pesa, a mobile payment system that is replicated in other parts of the world.

With a stable business environment, it is the choice of overseas companies looking to investigate the East African market for entry. Its shared borders with Ethiopia also provide ample opportunity for investors seeking to follow the Ethiopian Jewry to Ethiopia to take advantage of its rapidly growing economy. It is populated by people mainly from the tribes of Kikuyu, Luhya and Kalenjin, but the official languages are English and Kiswahili. They are predominantly Christians. It has an international airport and several universities, including the University of Nairobi. The local currency is the Kenyan Shillings.

Favorite sports include the long distance race, football, basketball and volleyball. It is renowned globally for its wildlife parks and safari. Indigenous foods include gali, nyama githeri and chapati.

Dress code is formal. Office hours are between 9:00 a.m. and 5:00 p.m., Monday to Friday. There is a flexible attitude to meeting times. Information on business is available at the Kenya Trade Network Agency.

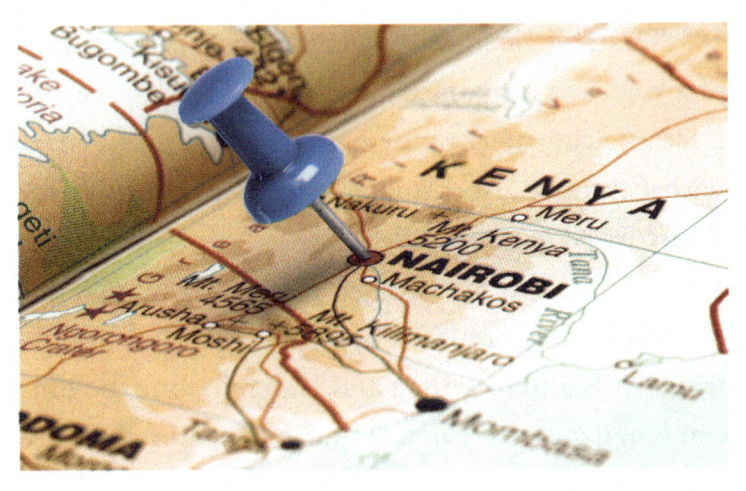

The United Arab Emirates (UAE)

The Emirates is outside of the African continent but prides itself as Africa's gateway. This may be seen as unusual but it has lived up to this for years. According to Daniel Kaufman of Norton, Rose and Fulbright Legal, Dubai is successfully positioning itself as the main international hub for trade with the African continent for reasons that include Dubai's unique geo-political position connecting Europe, Asia and Africa and its long-standing trading history as a strategic port on the Southern Silk Road. There is a big push for the UAE, the Chinese government and African governments to actually link the three regions together, reported *Euronews*, 28 November, 2019.

Dubai prides itself on good infrastructure, easy access to visas and Islamic finance. Its airline, Emirates, traverses the continent, moving people and business across cities. Hamad Buamim, president, Dubai Chamber of Commerce and responsible for the Global Business Forum on Africa is looking at different ways of working with businesses on the

African continent. According to him, Africa has uncertainties, certain risks, but also, appetite.

Africa is Now!

Majority of Israeli companies do not have Africa in mind when they set out to expand their operations abroad. It is not their first or even second overseas market consideration. This is clearly evident in the fact that Israel's exports to all the 54 countries in Africa adds up to less than 1% of its overall export, as Amit Levi, head of Israel's Economic Mission to South Africa, laments.

Africa, as the second largest and second most populous continent in the world, holds a lot of opportunities for Israeli companies, he notes.

Israel is not alone. Annalise Feller, in her report on rethinking Australia's approach to Africa, questioned the rationale behind the lack of understanding by Australian companies of the immense opportunities for trade and investment in Africa. According to her, while Australia's two-way goods and services trade to the entire continent of Africa was valued at $11.4b, the total value of trade with ASEAN countries was $105b.

Africa's potential as an emerging market remains underestimated. A report by the US Chamber of Commerce based on a boardroom survey of attitudes towards corporate investments in Africa noted that most companies require a strong and specific draw to make investment in Africa worthwhile. Africa is also grossly misunderstood, tainted by misconceptions and a reputation for risks, but in reality, default rates are often lower in Africa than elsewhere, reports the *Financial Times*. According to Moody's, this is less than 6% and half the default rate in Latin America.

The comforting news is, according to Israel's Amit Levi, the perception of businesses change quickly for the better as soon as they settle into the continent. Africans are genuinely hospitable and welcoming to visitors, and the longer the stay, the more the benefits. Unfortunately, not every entrepreneur has heard this gospel that business is good in Africa. To some investors, Africa is only one of the many possible destinations that they may consider for investment and in many cases, it is the least considered destination.

Over the years, experience has shown that many businesspeople are yet to fully understand the cultural nuances and the dynamics of doing business in Africa. Asides funding considerations, the fact that there are very few commercial outposts in the huge continent has not helped matters. Ostensibly, the report out of these outposts does not reflect the diversity of the continent.

Following the attention the continent is getting from the global business community and the recent normalization of ties between Israel, Morocco and Sudan, it has become imperative to guide entrepreneurs and investors in Israel on the 'where,' 'why' and the 'how' to do business in the emerging Africa. The reasons are not far-fetched:

A. A post-pandemic world creates the imperative for new markets.

B. Africa has the largest free trade area in the world and is open for business.

The continent that has been described as the final frontier is on its way to deliver on its enormous promise.

CHAPTER 2

Why Should You Do Business in Africa?

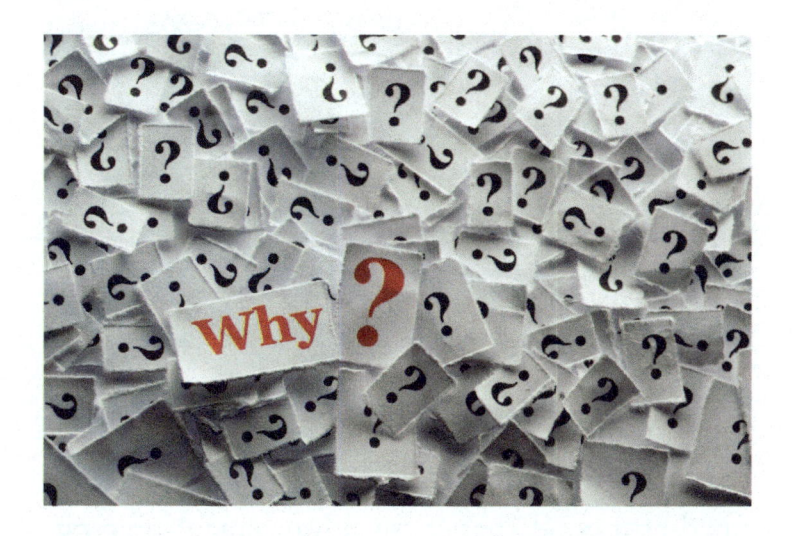

Africa is predicted to account for 25% of the world's population by 2050 and 40% by 2100. This is a source of optimism and economic opportunity! High economic growth rates combined with the world's youngest and fastest growing population fuels the optimism. However, Africa needs partners to attain its goal of socio-economic transformation.

The Opportunities

Opportunity is defined as a set of circumstances that make it possible to do something. It is also defined as a good chance for advancement or progress. The COVID-19 pandemic offers the world a once-in-a-generation chance to remake society and build a better future.

Africa is a Land of Opportunities

Acha Leke and Landry Signé, in a report published by Brookings Institution on succeeding in business in Africa (Leke and Signé 2019), listed five bold business opportunities that a discerning investor should be aware of and take advantage of.

Opportunity 1. *Africa has a huge population that is fast growing and urbanizing.*

According to the report, Africa's current population of 1.2 billion people is projected to reach 1.7

billion by 2030. Moreover, more than 80% of the population growth will occur in cities. Its youthful population and growing middle class is educated and speaks mostly English, French, Portuguese and Arabic, offering immense opportunities.

Africa is rapidly urbanizing and is home to 52 cities with more than one million people. This is phenomenal and holds a lot of promise for companies engaged in infrastructure development and urban services. According to McKinsey, 2021, by 2025, half of the biggest companies will be based in the developing world, many in fast-growing cities perhaps never heard of.

Opportunity 2. *Africa is industrializing.*

The report says that African industrial revolution is underway, from the processing of agricultural products to smart manufacturing. Although many African countries continue to benefit from traditional exports of oil, gold, diamonds, rubber and forest products, national governments are diversifying beyond these industries (Achour et al., 2015).

In an interview with Forbes Africa, May 2021, the managing director of GIADEC, Ghana's aluminium company, had this to say, 'We have been operating with a clear mandate to develop and promote the integrated aluminium industry in Ghana. Development means owning the full process from beginning to end, everything from the inception of the business idea to selecting partnerships and doing what is enduring in terms of the long-term value chain development of the aluminium industry. Promotion is about making sure that we continue to develop, promoting not just the market's capacity but assisting the comprehension of the industry stakeholders, communities and other interest groups.'

Opportunity 3. *Africa is pushing to close the infrastructure gap.*

A critical driver of economic and social progress for Africa is infrastructure development. The African Development Bank estimates that over $100 billion investment for at least 10 consecutive years is required to address the current infrastructure deficits on the continent.

Governments in Africa are therefore working tirelessly individually or in partnership with the private sector and multilateral agencies to provide infrastructure or to improve on the efficiency of existing utilities in transportation, energy, telecommunication, ports, dams, and etcetera. They seek increased engagement with the outside world for public private partnerships (PPP) in their quest for enhanced capital and expertise.

In a meeting, June 2021, the Group of Seven (G7) Development Finance Institutions (DFIs) and partners announced a commitment to invest $80 billion in Africa's private sector, over the next five years, to support sustainable economic recovery and growth in the continent. It is the first time the G7 DFIs have come together to make a collective partnership to the continent.

Opportunity 4. *Innovation to unleash agricultural and resource wealth.*

Subsistence agriculture is widespread in the continent but no longer tolerable, if the country must feed itself. Improved seedlings, modern farm equipment, herbicides, storage facilities and mills for food processing are necessary in the war against hunger. Concerted efforts are made by governments in the continent to support cutting-edge technologies to transform its agricultural, minerals and other resource endowments in order to create wealth.

Opportunity 5. *The potential of increasing digital and mobile access.*

In the absence of traditional landlines, Africa has leapfrogged in digital access by mobile telephony which requires less hard infrastructure. It has one of the fastest growing mobile access in the world and, with a staggering penetration rate of over 80% in some of its countries, creates favourable environments for startups and FinTech companies to develop and thrive, particularly with the rise in the use of smart phones. Mobile data tariff is expected to increase sevenfold by 2022.

Africa is the final frontier for communication technology disruption. This is demonstrated in the rapidity of deployment of broadband connections across the continent. Though broadband can be defined in many ways, it is generally understood to be a service that enables reliable, high speed transfer of data, voice and video over the Internet. According to a World Bank report, broadband is not just an infrastructure; it is a general purpose technology that can fundamentally restructure an economy and foster global competitiveness.

The benefits of broadband deployment in the provision and facilitation of government services, education, commerce, entertainment, healthcare, agricultural practices and law enforcement cannot be overemphasized. In a smart city environment, for instance, broadband networks enable police, fire and emergency medical personnel to reach crises more quickly. The challenges faced by practitioners in some of the African countries, for instance, Nigeria, include the lack of financing options, harsh regulatory conditions and the slow progress to deploying broadband Internet infrastructure.

In the opinion of Leke and Signé, although Africa's successful firms differ widely in their geographic and sector focus, the fastest-growing and most profitable businesses in Africa typically see challenges as a spur for innovation.

Unlocking the Opportunities

The challenge of weak infrastructure, such as in health service, exposed by the COVID-19 pandemic in several parts of the continent presents an opportunity for a discerning investor. Technology offers major disruption and a leapfrog for many African countries. The presence of educated youths adaptable to the knowledge economy is an opportunity to disrupt the traditional systems for improved delivery. Governments across Africa are aware of the advantage that technology offers in terms of efficiency and operational costs. These governments have moved to provide investors with enabling environments, including improvements in their ease of doing business, registration of companies, visas on arrival, tax holidays and pioneer status arrangements, investors protection, ease of funds repatriation, protection of intellectual property rights, good regulatory business environment and one-stop shop on foreign direct investments.

Investment Opportunities by Sector

Opportunities for investment in Africa are available in the following sectors:

Digital Health: COVID-19 pandemic and the attendant global lockdown exposed the weak health infrastructure in the entire continent, paving the way for urgent intervention in the administration of healthcare services. Virtual care solutions are making substantial impact and may have greater impact in rural and under-served environments through community medical and nursing facilities. According to a report released by McKinsey, May 8, 2020, new growth opportunities exist in tele-health consultations, home healthcare services, non-ER-based primary community care and more proactive regular remote behavioural health screening.

Agtech: The urgent need to feed the rapidly growing population of Africans indicates that subsistence agriculture is no longer sustainable. Modern technologies are needed to reduce post-harvest losses, manage water use, and improve crop yield, milk production and aquaculture, drones in agriculture, precision farming, and etcetera. Governments are interested in partnering with companies that are willing to go into joint ventures for aquaculture, livestock breeding and in the production of livestock feeds and fertilizers. These projects have the capacity to generate employment for the teeming youths, in addition to ensuring food security.

Cyber Security: In the emerging future of work, organizations will have to pay more attention to cyber security and take proactive steps to keep their operations safe from hackers, criminals and terrorists. Criminals exploit cyber security gaps to perpetrate havoc such as espionage and cross-country cyber-attacks, including picking up of ransoms. The dastardly efforts by criminals and terrorists to hack into computer infrastructure of financial institutions, health facilities, among others, and the sabotage of oil pipelines and power stations and such other installations call for increased digital security initiative and robust cyber protection, especially in the aftermath of the COVID-19 pandemic which has forced on line a significant portion of human activities.

According to Jason Ikogwu, Nigerian Vanguard Newspaper, June 13, 2021, multi-factor authentication (MFA) will be critical against cyber intrusion. Password spraying and credentials stuffing attacks will be on the rise and so organizations should make adequate preparations to implement different variants of multi-factor authentication. In the new normal, raised levels of cyber threats come with increasing use of cloud computing for remote work and online collaborations.

Edutech: It is the combined use of computer hardware, software, educational theory and practice to facilitate learning. National lockdowns arising from the COVID-19 have informed the need for virtual learning. Publishers of textbooks used in schools can convert their content into digital format. The application of artificial intelligence engines that analyse students' behaviour for the 21st century enables personalized learning experience, especially in the STEM subjects.

FinTech: Africa is under-banked. This is glaring in the rural areas, so disrupting traditional banking was necessary to ease the burden on consumers during payments and transfers. Necessity is the mother of invention. Kenyan M-Pesa which has set the pace for mobile payment across the world was born out of this need. There is a huge payment infrastructure gap across the continent but FinTech companies are filling the gaps.

Renewable Energy: Across the globe, nearly 800 million people live without access to electricity, about 600 million of them are in sub-Saharan Africa, says Timmermans and Birol in a special report on Al Jazeera, 17 June, 2021. The search for reliable sources of power continues, with many governments contemplating independent power plants (IPP), set up of small refineries and alternative sources such as wind, biogas and solar energy.

The world's drive to cut back on carbon emissions means that renewable energy will be the next big thing in the power game. However, in some countries, import of generating sets remains high as the population subscribes to any appliance that provides them with some semblance of regular power supply. Though in the long run, governments anticipate renewable and sustainable sources of energy development, any source of power is acceptable in the near term as homes and offices are in dire need of energy to power their air-conditioners, office equipment and industrial machines.

According to the FDI Intelligence, a service from

the *Financial Times*, May, 2021, solar energy may well be a green and cost-effective solution to the chronic power issues faced by many African countries, but its potential remains largely untapped across the continent.

In a 2020 report published by the World Bank, *Global Photovoltaic Power Potential by Country*, it highlights that, unlike Europe and North America which have considerable installed capacity but lower average rates of potential solar energy, many African countries have been beset by problems concerning the electricity grid, regulation and attracting capital, despite its huge reservoir of solar energy.

According to the Al Jazeera report, (*op. cit*) the barriers to deploying solar and other renewable technologies include the initial costs of installing them. Now, there are innovative pay-as-you-go business models to spread out the upfront costs. With cheap renewable and green investments, universal energy access will be possible by 2030, the year set by the International Energy Agency to end energy poverty in the world.

The European Union has jump started intervention with its Green Energy Initiative to provide grants, technical assistance and financial instruments to support investments in renewable energy generation across Africa.

Public Safety Emergency Response: As the use of mobile phones continues to grow in Africa, the number of emergency calls that potentially can be made are high. Today's mobile phones have the ability to provide emergency dispatch services called Public Safety Answering Points (PSAPs) with important information that they can transmit to call responders.

10,000 people lose their lives every year because first responders are not able to get accurate location information from emergency calls, according to Alex Dizengof, co-founder, Carbyne, a public safety emergency response company. A full ecosystem therefore, is far-reaching for cities that aspire to be smart and liveable, for which good public safety infrastructure is a sine qua non for attracting foreign direct investment, talent and skilled persons.

Infrastructure: The population of Africans in cities has been projected to increase in coming years. This would compromise public utilities such as housing, water supplies and electricity as carrying capacities would be exceeded. Investments in infrastructure, including roads, airports, seaports, and power plants are required to keep pace with demand and use.

Technology Incubation and Acceleration: The Fourth Industrial Revolution and the associated knowledge economy offers opportunities to set up technology incubators in cities, especially those with a talent pool, for instance, university towns. Private sector investment in technology ecosystems will raise the interest level, especially among the youths, in innovation and creative thinking.

Business Process Outsourcing: Educated youth, most of whom speak English and French, offer an opportunity for affordable business process operations which may include call centres, data entry and coding. Qualified software engineers can be recruited to offer back office services at convenient fees to overseas firms. Facilities to provide these services are opening in major cities across Africa.

Moreover, repatriates or returnee Africans from the Diaspora form a ready pool of skilled and experienced human resource for companies that seek best practice for their business. With exposure in management practice, healthcare, accounting, HR and schools, the expertise of repatriates is of immense value to companies considering the opportunities in the service sectors.

ICT and Data Centres: Countries in Africa have some of the fastest growing Internet markets but lack the necessary infrastructure. High-speed subsea cables are required to accelerate data transfer speeds, reports the Financial Times. There is an opportunity in public cloud services. Data centres would profit from the trend of working from home due to the COVID-19 lock-downs and its aftermath. Presently, a very large part of Africa's data warehouses are outside of the continent.

Knowledge Tours: Technology, a key component

of the knowledge economy, has taken centre stage, creating disruptions in hitherto traditional sectors through innovation and research. Many knowledge firms are believed to cluster around institutions of higher learning for easy access to talents. In partnership with African governments at various levels—federal, state and local council—youth with appreciable levels of education and in relevant disciplines can be offered internship positions and short-term training opportunities in technologically-advanced countries. Beneficiaries of these models of training are good candidates for engagement in smart manufacturing, drawing from knowledge acquired in data analyses, advanced robotics and deep learning.

Israel: The Game Changer

Israel's capacity for innovation has been identified as its main strength such that insecurity and other significant adverse conditions have not fazed the citizens of the country from digging deep into research and development. The World Economic Forum in its global competitiveness reports has consistently ranked Israel as a major player in the international economy. In a release by StartupBlink's *Global Startup Ecosystem Index Report*, 2021, Israel ranks 3rd among the global top 50 technology startups ecosystems with eleven ranked cities.

According to a report in the *Jerusalem Post*, 21 June, 2021, Israel also ranks 2nd globally in hardware and IoT, health technology, software and data industries and also ranks in the world's top 5 in energy and environment technology, marketing and sales technology and social and leisure technology. Among top 1000 technology cities surveyed, Tel Aviv, an Israeli city, ranked 8th behind San Francisco, New York, Beijing, Los Angeles, London, Boston and Shanghai. Other Israeli cities that made the top 1000 cities include Jerusalem (54th), Haifa (119th), Beer Sheva (238th), Yoknean (248th), Ashdod (459th), Eilat (474th), Nazareth (508th), Caesarea (521th), Modiin (627th) and Nahariya (914th).

In an email communication by Sherwin Pomerantz, president, Atid-EDI, one of Israel's top economic development consulting firms, he wrote, that based on data available to him, Israel's innovation technology sector broke a new capital funding, reaching a total of $10.5 billion raised since the start of 2021. In doing so, it matched the total raised throughout the whole of 2020—which was itself a record year—in less than half the time.

According to him, the bulk of funding went to cyber security, FinTech and enterprise solutions companies, with the top three sectors pulling an accumulated $6.2 billion or 60% of all investments. These sectors are all software, strongly B2B oriented, and saw huge increases in demand for their solutions over the last year as work practices changed. It attests to the continued vitality of Israel's tech sector at a time when the world has its concerns about the economic recovery after COVID-19, he noted.

I will paraphrase the words of Dan Senor and Saul Singer in their book, *Start-up Nation: The Story of Israel's Economic Miracle*. In this book, the authors note that Israel has something to offer that is sought by other countries, including countries that are considered to be on the forefront of global competitiveness. According to the authors, in addition to the institutional elements that make up clusters, which Finland, Singapore and South Korea already possess, what is missing in these other countries is a cultural core built on a rich stew of aggressiveness and team orientation, on isolation and connectedness, and on being small and aiming big.

The secret then of Israel's success is the combination of some classic elements of technology clusters with some unique Israeli elements that enhance the skills and experience of individuals, make them work together more effectively as teams and provide tight and readily available connections within an established and growing community.

Messrs Dan Senor and Saul Singer further noted

that while innovation is scarce, it is a renewable resource. Unlike finite natural resources, ideas can spread and benefit whichever countries are best positioned to take advantage of them, regardless of where they are invented. It is not a surprise that several countries including India, Singapore and South Korea have bilateral scientific and technological agreements with Israel. It is not a coincidence either that many global companies, including Google, Amazon, Microsoft, Intel, Facebook, Nestle, Merck, IBM, eBay, Cisco, Applied Materials, Apple, Barclays, Unilever, Citigroup, Dell, GE, Pfizer and etcetera seek out Israel for their research and development arms.

African governments and the private sector doing business with the UAE can seize the opportunity of the Abraham Accord signed between the Emirates/Gulf States and Israel to advance trade and investment. There are huge capital flows from the Emirates to Africa for infrastructure that Israeli technology firms can plug into. This is coming at a time when explosion of activities in the flow of Islamic finance and insurance into Africa is expected.

According to Daniel Kaufman in an edition of Inside Africa, 2016, for the law firm, Norton, Rose and Fulbright, Islamic Development Finance Institutions (DFIs)—many of which are based in the UAE—are working with a number of African countries to develop their legislative and regulatory frameworks to better support Islamic finance products for the future.

Bottlenecks

Despite these mouth-watering opportunities, there are challenges. According to Yael B, owner,

Mountain Goat Ventures, a US and Israeli business consultant and former Business Development Manager, Empower Africa, the concerns include the following:

- Challenges with hiring locally due to gaps in culture and work ethics.
- Lack of transparency in costs for foreigners versus locals.
- Time required to get projects done without caving into bribery
- Expensive to do business if corruption are rampant.
- Difficulty in navigating local stakeholders
- Existing competition that have strongholds on local stakeholders.

Aside from the red tape, especially in the public sector, there are blind spots that threaten to jeopardize successful navigation on the African business terrain. These include ethnic conflicts and religion crises. Nevertheless, efforts are made by respective governments to reduce or eradicate the issues that may forestall the growth of their respective economies. The various regions are working in tandem with the African Union and the UN to ensure peace in volatile regions. On economic crimes, there are commissions set up by governments to combat the menace and to prosecute the perpetrators.

For major infrastructure projects, corrupt practices by governments and others engaged in public private partnerships (PPP) can be nipped in the bud by having projects sponsored by Development Finance Institutions and similar multilateral agencies paid for at the source of funds.

CHAPTER 3

How to Enter Africa?

Africa is a continent with extraordinary challenges, but it has room for many investors and entrepreneurs. However, doing business in Africa must be driven by a deeper purpose that requires resilience. According to Amit Levi, Israel Commercial Office, Johannesburg, South Africa, doing business in Africa should be considered a long-term investment and adequate preparation is required.

Preparing for Success

Success in business can be compared to a breakthrough in sport. Richard Branson, founder, Virgin Group, speaking with Kathleen Elkins on a CNBC program, *Make It*, October 12, 2016, said that a lot of things he learned through sports are transferable to other aspects of life. 'I certainly found that the skills I have acquired playing tennis have been beneficial to my business career.'

Since dropping out of school at age 16 to start his first business, Branson has overseen hundreds of companies and accumulated a fortune of approximately $5 billion. Part of that success can be credited to the game of tennis, a sport that parallels the life of an entrepreneur, the Virgin Group founder wrote in a LinkedIn post, "Why Athletes Make Great Entrepreneurs."

'Tennis, like business, moves so quickly that if you dwell on the past for even a few minutes, an opportunity will have passed and the moment will be lost.' Branson explained, 'The mental side of tennis has always enormously appealed to me. While you have an opponent on the other side of the net, the most challenging adversary is yourself. You have to get into the right frame of mind in order to perform your best, and need to be able to put setbacks behind you instantly.'

The Inner Game of Tennis

Billionaire Richard Branson's observations finds expression in Timothy Gallwey's bestselling book, *The Inner Game of Tennis*. Timothy Gallwey defines winning as overcoming obstacles to reach a goal. According to him, there are two components of tennis (or any sport), namely an outer game and an inner game.

In Gallwey's opinion, we are already masters of the inner game which takes place in our minds. It is only a matter of unlearning the bad habits such as lapses in concentration, nervousness and self condemnation which are distractions that stop us on our tracks in the outer game.

The success of *The Inner Game of Tennis* by Timothy Gallwey inspired Pete Carroll to write a book, *The Inner Game of Success: An Inside-out Approach*.

According to Carroll, focus, clarity and belief in yourself are what allow you to express your ability without discursive thoughts and concerns. His deductions are that success arises from three resourceful inner states: Awareness. Choice. Trust

- Awareness: Understanding the present situation with clarity of purpose.
- Choice: Moving in the direction desired for the future.
- Trust: Reliance on the inner self as the essential link to dealing with the external world where the outer self resides.

Preparation is Key

The Chicago Council on Global Affairs published an article titled AFRICA IS NOW: The Opportunity for mid-sized US Companies in which a framework known as the PAL Principles was recommended for successful African market entry.

Be	• Prepared
Be	• Adaptive
Be	• Local

(A) Be prepared

According to the PAL principles, the unique opportunities and challenges of each African country make determining where to enter a new market and what strategy to use especially important. Company options may vary depending on the industry segment, the operations of the business environment, risk level and the political climate. An investor has to get their feet wet. A short visit to the host country would help your understanding of the local business culture while the face-to-face meeting would engender trust between the parties. In the new normal and with the adoption of virtual meetings and conferences, a visit is still encouraged. Plan to join a trade mission or a sector business delegation.

(B) Be adaptive

According to the report, there are a lot of things you have no choice but to adapt to in your host country. The frank advise is that a company needs to be able to adapt to the host environment rather than trying to mould it to suit your organization. You may have the shock of your life to find out that a couple of things taken for granted in your home country may be lacking in the host country. Infrastructure like roads and consistent access to electricity is often less than ideal and regulations sometimes change with the election of new political leaders. The irony is that business still thrives on the continent and smart managers figure out a way around these obstacles.

Consider yourself to be in it for the long haul. Strategies may need to change from the original plan based on changing operating environment such as different customer preferences, unwritten requirements of doing business, delays in getting business approvals or a sudden change in government policy, or widening infrastructure gaps.

(C) Be local

Successful businesses know that their ability to compete in any market depends on the people they employ and do business with. It may take the form of a merger/acquisition, greenfield, licensing, joint venture partnership or by appointing distributors to gain access to the market. However, even if a company does not require a local footprint, it will need to work with reliable local partners that can assist in navigating the market to properly execute the company's strategy. Local partnership provides significant advantages such as in-depth market knowledge, access to networks for financing, human capital and the ability to manoeuvre within local legislations. Local partners are critical to business success in Africa.

Building a reputation at the outset as a company that wants to work with local businesses helps to establish relationships that promote acceptance and support. Companies may have to build relationships with local village leaders, country directors, local trade associations, grass-root politicians and join local business clubs and charities like Rotary International. Influencers command a lot of respect within communities and can help to reduce the length of red tape in doing business. Engage them where appropriate.

In the course of writing this book, I had virtual interviews with some business development professionals. One of them was Shifka Seigel, project manager, Israel, Australia, New Zealand and Oceania Chamber of Commerce. Seigel offers the following advice to entrepreneurs venturing into new markets overseas:

- Research the market
- Be open-minded
- Be flexible
- Be straightforward
- Find partners

Efe Itoje, Managing Director, Turi International, and a UK-based entrepreneur with vast Nigeria experience shared some nuggets as fundamental to market entry:

- Good knowledge of the opportunities in the country through research.
- Find persons of influence to navigate the often-times difficult terrain.
- Reduce the liability of foreignness by working with a local partner.

Identifying Local Partners

Local partners are individuals and organizations that provide business services in locations you wish to conduct business. Even with on-site work, executing successful market entry strategies often requires a permanent local presence or partnership with a local entity.

A local partner should be a trusted local with a good knowledge of the industry and the geographical location. Such locals can be reached through the following:

- Desktop research through social media such as LinkedIn.

- Referral from the embassy of your country or host country.
- Referral from the city chamber of commerce.
- Host country's investment/trade promotion agency.
- Referral from other companies operating in host country
- Community of expatriates.
- Africa diaspora
- Market entry strategy advisors

Market entry strategy advisors bring expert insights into market entry processes and help companies to evaluate, understand and seize new market opportunities. Market entry strategic advisors assist you with on the ground connections to:

- Know the market.
- Build networks.
- Grow a sustainable business.

Working with an international market entry strategy advisor ensures the right market and consumer data is available during the decision-making process. According to MConsulting Prep, three questions are crucial to market entry decisions:

- Should I enter?
- Can I enter?
- How do I enter?

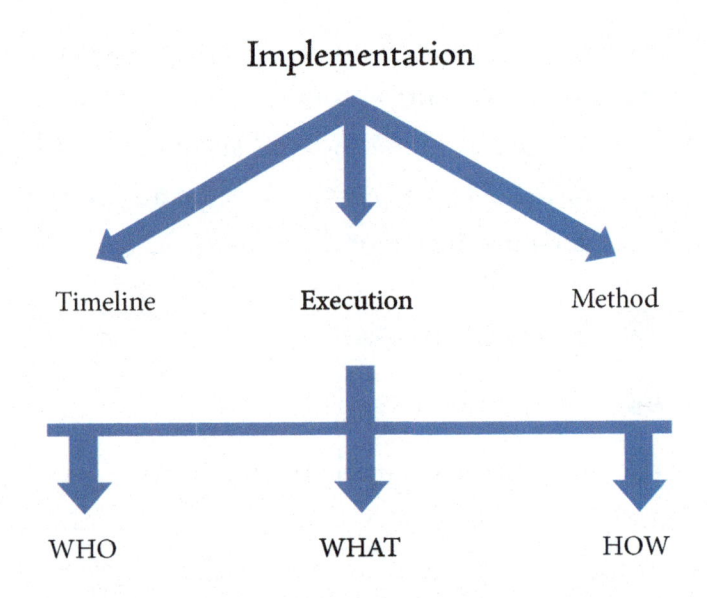

```
                    Implementation
                   ↙      ↓      ↘
            Timeline   Execution   Method
                   ↓      ↓      ↓
                 WHO    WHAT    HOW
```

Adapted from McPrep Market Entry Framework

CHAPTER 4

Hard Facts About Easy Market Entry

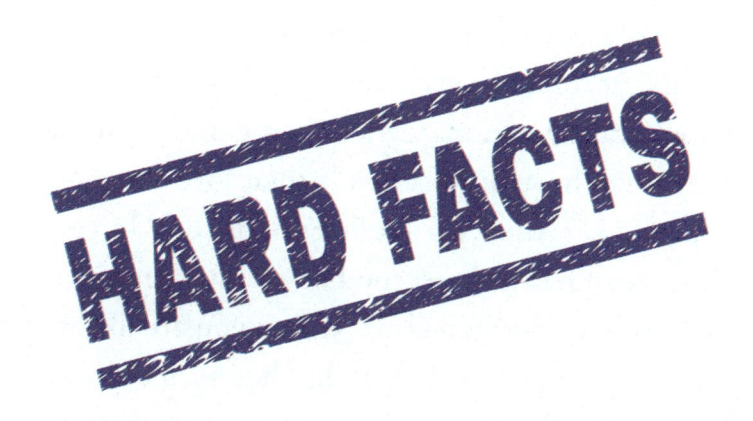

Africa is a continent of 54 countries and ways of doing business vary from country to country, region to region and even between rural and urban spaces. As noted in *Africa Now*, a report prepared by the Chicago Council on Global Affairs for mid-sized US Companies, there is no rule book to execute the perfect strategy. Nevertheless, several tips, facts and principles are recommended to help companies to implement their best strategies. However, there are some hard facts that a discerning business owner expanding into the continent should be aware of. Some of them are considered here:

Culture: Africa is a huge mix of culture and traditions. The manner of greeting, keeping appointments, negotiation styles and perspectives vary by tribes and by region. Generally, a common thread that runs through Africans is their love for people expressed in their hospitality to visitors. In some cases, love has to be earned as many Africans, especially the educated class (whom you are likely to meet), feel that their hospitality has been exploited in the past through their experience of colonization. Do not take it for granted.

According to the Ethiopian country resource person on cross-cultural training programs for DFA Global International Solutions, USA, investors and entrepreneurs are often advised to have an open mind as they learn more about the culture of the country where they are about to start doing business. Though the traditional way of life may have been altered in certain ways by their colonial heritage and history, aspects of indigenous cultural traits persist. Africans abhor arrogance. Majority frown at lewd remarks and indecent exposures. African names have meanings. Build relationships by trying to know the meanings of the names.

Talk sports. Africans love sports. Research the major sports and pastime in the city and country. Know the names of local sports heroes. It endears you to the locals when you talk glowingly about their sports heroes. Local business people are ready to engage in lengthy chats about international sports of interest. Do not dabble into political and religious matters. Do not fuss over their lateness to meetings. Many are working hard to correct the use of the so-called 'African time.'

Investors would do well to bring with them their positive life experiences to ensure that the people they are working with benefit from these experiences. Improve working conditions to uplift the living standards of the local staff and community. It is a legacy cherished by many Africans.

Media: It has a far-reaching implication on the nature of news broadcast about the continent. Breaking news are usually negative and issues are hyped to suit the traditional audience, usually outside the continent. Generally, media reporting on Africa tend toward wars, poverty, sickness, hunger, totalitarian regimes, abuse of fundamental human rights and the flouting of the rule of law in many nations across the continent. Of course, this is not the entire picture.

Thanks to social media, it is now possible to seek a balance of information from disparate sources, despite the prevalence of fake news. To mitigate the influence of media bias and bad press on your decision making concerning the continent, read news from established and reputable media houses and validate information by contacting your embassy in the host country, or other nationals working in the host country.

Language: In most countries in Africa, English, French, Spanish and Portuguese are the languages of business. While it may not be necessary to understand the indigenous languages to do business, learning a few words in the local language, for instance, greetings and compliments, will certainly be door openers. Do not learn uncomplimentary words. It can be offensive to some people, especially the religious ones. Try to be politically correct in your discussions with locals. Do not leave the feeling that you are offering help. In business contexts, use words like 'partnership' and 'collaboration' instead of words like 'help' and 'assistance.'

Institutions: Legal institutions in many African countries are legacies from their colonial past. With a little tweak, the administration of justice are fashioned after the legal systems in Europe. However, there have been major reforms in many countries to cover intellectual property rights, repatriation of funds and economic crimes. The slow implementation of e-government creates loopholes exploited in the civil service. Business registrations may be slow in some of the countries but do not take the bait to undercut the system. Do not give any bribe to expedite the process. It is unlawful. The good news is that many foreign governments have policies on gift giving and bribes in general.

History: Majority of African countries were under the colonial rule of Britain and France. While the British governed most of its territories through indirect rule, the French system of government was assimilation. These differing systems of government have repercussions on Africa's relations with governments of former colonial administration, their economy and law.

Market size: The decision of any company to enter international trade and investment is mainly first, economic, which translates to profit making as the bottom line. As such, the size of the market, which is a function of population size and disposable income, is often a critical factor. Population varies by country. It is recommended that population be analysed in relation to the product sector and that the demographics of potential buyers be known before taking a dive into a market.

Connectivity: Today's businesses are powered by efficient communication networks. With reduced travel imposed by lockdowns, telecommunications networks and availability of Internet connections, and especially broadband connectivity, are important. You must ensure that your host city has Internet connection and WIFI in hotels. Some of the popular networks in Africa include MTN, Airtel and Vodacom. 5G network roll-out is slow but in progress in some parts of the continent. Availability of co-working spaces is also an essential in today's business tool-kit.

Travel: Travelling is smoother, more convenient and cheaper with fewer transfers. Check if the city of choice has a direct connection to your home city. One or two stops is generally considered fine in international business travel. What is the time zone? It is important to arrive in cities with airports or close to airports in order to avoid arduous local land travel by road, rail or water transport. Transport infrastructure, safety and security should be of utmost concern. Many governments in Africa have introduced visa on arrival for business travellers as an incentive.

Political Climate: Most countries in Africa practice parliamentary democracy, therefore, in principle, the rule of law applies. However, there are pockets of countries with despotic and sit-tight rulers. Political reforms are rare in such countries. Moreover, such environments give room to uprisings and revolts against the incumbent government, especially where sham elections to mirror democratic elections are conducted.

In some countries, the unequal distribution of wealth results in restiveness, especially among the youth, clamour for independence and communal wars for the control of natural resources. There have been cases of xenophobia, especially where the economy of the host country plummets. These environments are not safe for a foreign investor so it is advisable to seek security update and intelligence reports on the political situation in any country of proposed visit and investment.

Hard Facts About Easy Market Entry

Further Reading

Acha Leke and Landry Signe (2019): Spotlighting opportunities for business in Africa and strategies to succeed in the world's next growth market, Brooking Institution, January 11.

Achour I, Bader B, Shelleman R, Wilburn K, Thomas L, Unnikrishman S, (2015): Africa is Now: The Opportunity for Midsized US Companies. The Chicago Council on Global Affairs, Emerging Leaders Perspective. June\

Baird F (2021): Africa for Sale. Baird's CMC. www.bairdscmc.com

Carroll Pete: Inner Game of Success: An Inside-Out Approach. Review by Santosh Babu, BusinessToday. In, August 08, 2021.

Casablanca Finance City (2021): Your Business Partner for Africa's Potential. www.casablancafinancecity.com

CIA (2021): World Factbook. August 5. www.cia.gov

Elkins Kathleen (2016): The Definitive Guide to Business. Billionaire Richard Branson: The critical business lesson I learned from playing tennis. CNBC Make It. https://www.cnbc.com/2016/10/11/billionaire-richard-branson-the-critical-business-lesson-i-learned-from-playing-tennis.html

Feller Annalise (2021): Rethinking Australia's Appraoch to Africa. Fresh Perspective. Australian Institute of International Affairs, May 7

Florida R, Adler P and Mellander C (2016): The city as an innovative machine. Working paper series. Martin Prosperity Research.

Forbes: Africa (2021) Africa Undiscovered Series, April/May edition.

Gallwey W. Timothy (2015): The Inner Game of Tennis: The Ultimate Guide to the Mental Side of Peak Performance, Pan Macmillan

Gardham Richard (2021): Is Africa Finally On The Road To Prosperity? Investment Monitor, Eye on FDI. June

Kaufman David (2016) Dubai. Gateway to Africa. Norton Rose and Fulbright Law, Inside Africa Blog, June 15.

Levi Amit (2020): Israeli tech companies should treat South Africa as a springboard to whole continent. www.calcalistech.com, June 22.

MConsulting Prep (2021): Everyone can make it to consulting. www.mconsulting.com

McKinsey Global Institute (2021) The future of work after COVID-19. www.mckinsey.com

NoCamels (2019): Over 500 Global Corporations From 35 Countries Operate in Israel. April www.nocamels.com

Pilling David (2021): African Start-ups Attract International Investors But Need Local Ones Too. Financial Times, www.ft.com. July 15

Senor Dan and Singer Saul (2011): The StartUp Nation, The Story Of Israel's Economic Miracle. Little Brown and Company, London, USA.

StartUp Blink (2021): The Global Startup Ecosystem Index Report. www.startupblink.com

World Bank (2020): Global Photovoltaic Power Potential by Country. World Bank Group.

About the Author

Ndudi Osakwe is a market entry advisor, business research consultant and spatial analyst. His market research and consulting experience span over 25 years serving as the Nigerian country representative of the US State of Missouri Office for International Marketing, east Mediterranean region, to the setting up of an independent office to meet with the needs of firms and government agencies that seek partnerships in Africa and Nigeria in particular. He offers location intelligence and provides support to firms in navigating the often-complex terrain of the African regulatory agencies by pointing them in the right direction.

Ndudi Osakwe's research activities are focused on a wide range of sectors, including agribusiness, financial services, healthcare, clean energy, mining, homeland security, education, smart manufacturing, retail and ICT. He provides services to local and state governments to showcase their destinations for regional economic development. His consultancy, Infoplus Business Research Services, assists firms with field surveys and spatial analyses across the African continent.

Made in the USA
Columbia, SC
05 August 2022